KNOWING THIS HAS CHANGED MY ENDING

First published in 2018
by Offord Road Books

www.offordroadbooks.co.uk

Typeset by Martha Sprackland
Printed in the UK by Palace Printers

All rights reserved © Alex MacDonald, 2018

The right of Alex MacDonald to be identified as author
of this work is asserted in accordance with Section 77
of the Copyrights, Designs and Patents Act 1988

ISBN 978–1–999–93044–8

1 3 5 7 9 10 8 6 4 2

Knowing This Has Changed My Ending

ALEX MACDONALD

My Friend, Blood Shaking My Heart

I have come close to it. I have felt peculiar
in the tree's serenade, the mosquito's song.
In Prague, it came slowly as morning shade,
watching the beggars with their elbows flat
on cobbles, their heads tucked in, the shame
of who they were in the rain, their melting cups.
And the sandy coat dogs tethered to black poles
outside betting shops, with hereditary milky eyes
that watch my hand pull back. When I am in
the suit swathe of the city, I am not myself.
Or when I saw the tenement's bathing woman
statue, bloody-nosed, NO BREAK painted
across her chest, I forgot who I was. I have held
the ordnance survey hands of women recalling
flowers, and I have slept beside forgotten
daughters of wealthy Americans. It leaves,
eventually, and I am left with something worse,
thinking about my day ahead of me, feeling just fine.

Do Your Thing

Love you sleep well like a dachshund
kidney-bean shaped in diminishing z z z
now putting on your clothes
I want to dress just like you
shirt collar and cuffs and New Age necklace
our love is so androgynous
French-plaiting your hair when it unknots
its colour could blind the weak
our love makes us run past the eye hospital
your laugh is like an opera libretto
and the translation is 'love' in capitals
both your eyes are emerald tables
we're having our egg lunches on
and now you're heading for the stage door
to become the Viking of 6th Avenue
with a cat stepping between your helmet horns
when will I see you again until tonight
my beautiful Danish Prince?

Fine and How Are You

The woods mean something to everyone, even if it's nothing.
Trees prefer to stay together, to turn unanimously.
It's complicated, but I'm glad things actually happen.

No one mentions the many dinghies bobbing
in slow water, manned by bleached skeletons,
or vague mountain peaks dotted with stiffs
in fluorescent zip-wear.

We are often neatly side by side, a market stall selling
old remote controls, their subtle differences
conferring similar desires, to be precise, to be quiet,
to recall what has just happened.

A brain will fan like an orange only a handful of times,
open and wanting to be looked in to. How unfair
to call something timeless. You can lose yourself
in people and be undeniably present.

An Appreciation of Real Life

Outside of the bus's crazy window
I saw the world as it ought to be
and ate an ice cream in the shape

of Halloween eyeballs. I didn't check
the season. Old friends jousted
with outstretched hands, mortally

wounding each other with stories,
and discarded wigs dried out
on a bus-stop roof. You can tell a lot

about someone from their recycling
but there's a code, put this box next to
these beer cans, it's practically

a computer, it's basically anything.
By this point of my journey, I'd thought
of all the email addresses that I've occupied,

sitting on them like a glamorous toad.
The roads have a memory haze, showing
we are all capable of great things.

Gigantic Days

What days we're having now, with no vanishing point
and time like fat snakes rubbing against our ankles,
where I can feel the breeze and know myself.

In days I find my limits, a coral reef with fuzzy life.
How terrible it must be to have opinions
when so much is fresh conjecture.

Let's say I wake up inside a morning, wanting to be
more than table silence, to hold a friend's apple heart.
Shade reaches through the basement of my head.

I keep to alleyways, the rumbling cats. So often toast
is just warm bread, when it could be so hopeful.
There are no unknown fears.

I'm watching variations on the horizon, remembering
the horses and their complicated horse lives,
their shoes nailed on.

Days become a series of rooms. Wherever I sleep
a man is at my window. He tells me of days to come,
my calendar of question marks.

Don't Let Me Down, Important Spectacle

My drenched suit clings like a funeral mood
at what is now my third speech to the Board.

It's May and I dream of it ending, how a weatherman
might dream of weather unrepresented by symbols.

Everything relies on the photocopies I've handed out.
What invites faith – that yeasty smell, a flowerbed

in soft earth, my love with guinea-pig eyes, sadly looking?
I shift my weight from my bad leg to my overachieving leg.

My audience are adolescent boys at the front door
and Dad hasn't been home for years. Will I give them

jacket colognes, purple silks, the complicated futures?
I have seen tomorrow's forecast. It's clouds.

Lately I've Been Having Mine

Better to try and be perfect,
to search for love's flamingo legs,
bending however it helps
to stand in the amber
snake water. Our affections are waiting
for somewhere else.

After Hagiwara

I. *Blossom of the cul-de-sac*

Cherry blossom, this was to be your destiny, to scatter
your confetti on a conga line of drunk wheelie bins
at the entrance to this dead end.

I must have been staring too long, because faces greeted me
with smiles lit by birthday candles. 'What do you think
you're doing?' Ah, isn't it difficult to answer when neighbours
stand together like pylons in their small front gardens.

Birds top telephone poles and shine like spilled petrol,
the forecourt mirrors. Those masts stand taller than you,
gentle tree, as your petals rest on lumpy sacks like apologies.

II. *Graveyard at Home*

When cleaning my small home, I came across a graveyard
of ladybirds. Their dry bodies I mistook for amber jewels.
I am now rich with insect corpses. How funny that a community
of tragic husks has congregated in the shade underneath my chair,
asking nothing of me, laying on their backs baring their eyelash legs.
My heart is full of you, my previous tenants.

Hungerford Bridge

I'm thinking more about breaking
and what it means to crack my eggs.
I want to throw a glass against a wall
and watch it with intensity, then say
'Well, what do you think of that?' or
'Oh! Youth', anything to make a point.

Like the other week, I was standing
on a bridge in postman's weather.
The water sang in the way rivers do,
but this was sweeter than normal.
I heard the song it chose for me
and a plug was pulled somewhere
in my body, in a red darkness.

I was lonely as a bomb-disposal robot.
The song returns with its familiar hooks.
My masseuse said I should live
in the present. 'Are you
always this tense?'

New Lightness

A cento made from promotional emails from COS, a clothing company

In the extended quiet, the minimal sneaker details
our latest spring. Tokyo florists discover
the space-age and curious season textures.

New essentials cooperate splendidly with
traditional methods. The wardrobe is moonlit
on your return, a hand extended in the inky black
with something special to give you.

Our men swear, are quiet, are rounded shapes
in leather. We relax, wrap up our modern midnight.
Find something special with subtle hints
of the unexpected. Discover the chosen missing piece.
You can now enjoy our extra-soft neck, our reflective finish.

Kingfisher Days

It's difficult to love with a well-thumbed mind.
I deny myself hypothetical situations.
Even if I did escape, where would I go?
We are swallowed by country.

Shirtless, he looks for dead leaves and puts
them in my hand like he's paying me
for a day's work.

Packing away her child's toys, my sister said
that I need to listen to myself more.
Her wind-up phone with a smiley face is broken.

All I seem to do is drink milk from my favourite glass,
which was once a jar of fig jam. When he came home
and found me naked in the greenhouse, he was quiet
in his oversized shirt. He was somehow in there.

I'll find some standing water in a field, leading
to a floated meadow. Here I can give myself an image
of someone like me, breaking with light. The hurried
bodies of nature behind me. Birds arriving, then leaving.

Forever, Watching Love Grow

Something is flourishing in this waiting.
The still seat opposite, my boredom.

Punctuality is something you appreciate
late in life, when friends turn to tree stumps

and the under-floor heating is all hard water.
I wish I could grow a beard to make your arrival

more regal or, at least, a joke about how long
I have been sitting here. Each minute is greener

than the next, your face in strangers, that bowl
of flowers looks so familiar. I will not eat

but debone each thought, looking for the darker
meat, uncooked blood. My wooden restlessness.

I have ordered water six times and see the dirt
collecting on the floor. I wonder if we even made plans?

Did I force you to feed the birds? I've looked longingly
at your seat the way others look on travel websites.

I feel the heat on my back and all the salads are growing
warm. The restaurant lights go off and, inevitably,

I'm lifted from you and I didn't need to say anything.

You Are Most Welcome

In my message house, I'm busy erasing. Freedom used to be important, living the underwear life with better views, each window snowglobing, every sapling hamming it up. Any moment I could be rolling in love with gnarled lobsters. But on the hallway floor, I felt their pinch.

I became a regrettable character and my books grew dusty moustaches. I envied the accordionist's dog – it was so loyal and spooked. I said *oops* out loud when I dropped a knife, a starter, an elderly cat. Friends recommended songs called 'For No One' and 'Events in Dense Fog' that sounded like night-time deserts, a deep blue of the water denied them.

Let me be a reminder of white shirts drying in fields with husky bees. But if my choices make you hug someone you love tighter, so you can feel their skeleton, you are most welcome.

From 'Internet Cats'

These poems are named after different Instagram Japanese cat profiles. The text is a collage of the translated captions which accompanied the top 15 posts of those profiles

Dooboo Cat

Good night, I am the youngest of this house
and I am drying my sister, taking pictures
with that funny look and love is on the corner.
Today is a good friend, the world in itself.
I worry so much, help me, a man called Tofu
spread the things you put in the comments.
It's not good. Followed by a Saturday rotation,
you are my vitamin. I've collected a lot of beard
in a box with my mother eyes, I've seen only beard
and got a headache. Is there a god making me sick?

Rina Takei

A cold comes every night on top of me sleeping,
even sleeping between my legs, which is nice.
It did not strike a betrayal. I don't want him.

I like the smell of bread, what my husband was.
For the first time, Autumn, behold
this model-like expression.

Uncle wipes the window a lot, although it didn't
need cleaning. To be is a mystery. I was cleaning
my uncle in the home of the desired.

Now it's time for bed. The eyes in the back of my head
pretend I have a window at the side of me
where you were staring at yourself.

This Modern Life

I've been trying to open
the same bag of nuts
for the past year

that's what I thought
they were before this
wrapping wore away

I can't get what I'm getting at
but I'm open to reflections
what a hall of mirages

I must be loopy from how
cut and dry things have
become here

there's not a clown in the sky
and where's that rustling
coming from

what is it I dreamed of alone
candescent pillows and
a desire to dream better

No Clipping

*'Noclip' is the common name given to the cheat in videogames
which enables a player to walk through walls*

Last week I was a private detective and handcuffed all the corpses
for an Easter egg. This made me feel important, but it was my birthday.

A boy at school told me there's a way to access all levels: ice planet,
abandoned Valentine's Day warehouse, the President's car. Yesterday

I was stuck in the haunted hospital and I'm supposed to collect something.
I've looked under the children's pillows, spoken to my dying grandmother

ten times, but nothing. Sometimes I get tired and cheat. There is a way
I can walk through walls and see each room: kitchen, fake bathroom,

secret air vent. The object of the game is to get through the day
without being seen. But the army saw me and I died three times.

In another life, I built my dream house: fortress-like, filled with art
and photos of my husband. I discussed muffins with my neighbour

as our cooker burned everything and shaded my lover a red hue.
Did we have a baby? I couldn't save it. Today I'm being shot at

in the space prison, the pig policeman has good aim. I helped out
a prostitute inmate by running over her deadbeat customer.

She gave me the mansion's greenhouse key. When I inspect it closely
there is blood in the ridges. Knowing this has changed my ending.

End Space

I will write while the light is good   I have been asked to write
   in a room like this you think of the hiding places first
secret drawers   dusty chairs behind metal shutters   there is a smell
of medicine in the air   but I do not look sick   I look great
from this window I can see empty hospital beds lined up against
the sea wall   yellowing pillows   I have been asked to not think too hard
and if I do want to think it should be something from this help book
the examples   'your childhood pet'   'meadows covered in mist'
'different coloured wigs'   'spring flowers'

today I went on a walk   my third this week   I found the tennis courts
with the racquets lined up like machine guns   I played a few rounds solo
   hitting the ball against the wall wasn't that fun   the sound echoing
from the cobweb corners   when I found the pool it was a mirror
I wanted to swim   but instead I looked down on the patterned ceiling
   I went outside for the first time   I saw how the branches of the trees
were held back by wire to teach them their shape   there is a church here
   with a sign that reads   'No service'   who is watering my plants at home?
my brain feels dirty   as if it has grown a beard   I want to wake up very early

to see how the day changes   so I could say to someone   'well, it was much nicer earlier'   but I feel slow   I haven't seen anyone for a while   my bones feel like broken water   and when I stand on the beach I can see sirens along the coast held tightly with rust I wonder why they are there and then it starts   I think of the out of season holiday camps that we visited the wide waters   I remember the way you held your ice cream cone your amphitheatre fingers   I think of how each new building has designs to stop people from jumping off them   steel netting   impossible ledges there are people that spend their lives seeing men and women in flower beds

and garden them   I can't see anyone by the time I find my room again standing by the window   a few beds are still out there   I reach for the book and read out the prompts   'snow-capped mountain peaks'   'smaller babies' 'a sink filled with water and wine glasses'   'empty white bird houses'

Necessary Feeling

If you're reading this then I've finally given in
to the suspicions, or the roads have grown
more dangerous, or the parks too dark at night.

I gave up the people who knew me for mystery,
their whereabouts a moon that doesn't set
in my head. Everything I've said

has been an audience aside, addressing
the many-eyed black space to infer another's flaw,
my own boredom, vigorous love.

It's traditional to be full of wisdom but I'm tired.
I didn't get eyes with igneous hammocks
without pulling a few late-night boners.

The sheet music is in the bedside drawer.
It's open to interpretation but I play it
with a light sombre – think medieval ice-cream van.

This is probably more than you need.

Acknowledgements

Several of these poems are titled after song lyrics, including 'Do Your Thing' by Moondog, 'Sweedeedee' by Michael Hurley, 'Ceremony' by Joy Division and 'Cowboy' by Underworld.

'Gigantic Days' is named after the René Magritte painting *Les Jours Gigantesques*. 'Kingfisher Days' is inspired by a series of photos by Caitlin Duennebier. 'End Space' is named after an exhibition of Daniel Libeskind's architectural drawings; it was commissioned by Wendy Maclean for the 'Rest' show at Lion and Lamb Gallery and it was inspired by the painting *Interior Sequence* by Freyja Wright.

I am grateful to the editors of the following publications where some of these poems originally featured: *Ambit*, *The Best British Poetry* 2015 (Salt Publishing), *Elephant Magazine*, *MINERVA*, *The Next Review*, *PAIN*, *Poetry London*, *Queen Mob's Teahouse*, the *Quietus*, the *Rialto*, *Roulade,* and *The Scores*. I am also grateful to the Society of Authors for an Eric Gregory Award in 2016 and the Poetry School for all their support and encouragement.

Thank you to Rachael Allen, Emily Berry, Crispin Best, Julia Bird, Amy Blakemore, Sam Buchan-Watts, Dominic Bury, Jen Calleja, John Clegg, Joey Connolly, Edward Doegar, Laura Elliott, Sinead Evans, S. J. Fowler, Emily Hasler, Wayne Holloway-Smith, Sarah Howe, Amy Key, Rachel Long, Roddy Lumsden (and his Wednesday group), Kathryn Maris, Andrew McMillan, Faye McNulty, Andrew Parkes, Sophie Pearce, Rebecca Perry, Sam Riviere, Declan Ryan, Richard Scott, Angus Sinclair, Karl Smith, Francine Toon, Jack Underwood, Mark Waldron, Chrissy Williams and Jane Yeh.

Special thanks go to my parents, to Martha Sprackland and Patrick Davidson Roberts for their generosity, and to Felicity Hammond for the cover.